Cheetahs

Laura Marsh

NATIONAL GEOGRAPHIC

Washington, D.C.

For Granny
- L. F. M.

Design by Yay Design

Paperback ISBN: 978-1-4263-0855-0
Hardcover ISBN: 978-1-4263-0856-7

CO = Corbis; GI = Getty Images; IS = iStockphoto.com; NP = naturepl.com; NGS = NationalGeographicStock.com; MP = Minden Pictures; SS = Shutterstock; cover, Chris Johns/NGS; 1, Manoj Shah/GI; 2, Michael Poliza/GI; 4 (top), Frans Lanting/CO; 4 (center), Roman Kobzarev/IS; 4 (bottom), Andrew Dowsett/S; 5, ZSSD/MP; 6 (left), Eric Isselée/SS; 6 (right), Eric Isselée/SS; 7 (top left), Panoramic Images/GI; 7 (top right), Hedrus/SS; 7 (left center), Jonathan and Angela/GI; 7 (right center), Frans Lanting/CO; 7 (bottom left), Jonathan and Angela/GI; 7 (bottom right), Ivica Drusany/SS; 8 (left), Eric Isselée/IS; 8 (center), Eric Isselée/IS; 8 (right), Eric Isselée/IS; 8 (background), Gregor Schuster/GI; 9 (top), istvanffy/IS; 9 (bottom), Splurge Productions, Inc./GI; 10-11, Andy Rouse/NP; 12, Art Wolfe/GI; 13, Federico Veronesi/GI; 14, Martin Harvey/GI; 15, Anna Omelchenko/IS; 16-17, Tom Soucek/Verge/CO; 18 (top), Suzi Eszterhas/MP; 18 (bottom), Chris Johns/NGS; 19, Suzi Eszterhas/MP; 20-21, Suzi Eszterhas/NP; 22 (top), Albie Venter/SS; 22 (center), Suzi Eszterhas/MP; 22 (bottom), Suzi Eszterhas/MP; 23 (top), Federico Veronesi/GI; 23 (bottom), Acinonyx Jubatus/NP; 24, DAE Picture Library/GI; 24-25 (background), krechet/SS; 25, Robert Harding/GI; 26, Winfried Wisniewski/CO; 28-29, Martin Harvey/Alamy; 30, Acinonyx Jubatus/MP; 31, Suzi Eszterhas/MP; 32 (top left), Art Wolfe/GI; 32 (top right), Simon King/NP; 32 (left center), Federico Veronesi/GI; 32 (right center), Francois Van Heerden/IS; 32 (bottom left), Suzi Eszterhas/NP; 32 (bottom right), Francois Van Heerden/IS

Printed in the United States of America
(SC) 12/WOR/4
(RLB) 12/WOR/3

Table of Contents

It's a Cheetah!

What runs so fast
it races by in a flash?

What looks
like it cries
but has no
tears in
its eyes?

What is covered in spots
and lives where it's hot?

4

It's a cheetah! (And we're not "lion.")

Cheetahs are large cats that look as cute and cuddly as a house cat. But you wouldn't want to snuggle up to a cheetah!

Cheetahs are powerful hunters with sharp claws and teeth.

Spotting Cheetahs

Cheetahs and leopards look alike because they both have spots. But they are different in many ways.

Cheetahs have "tear marks." These are black stripes that run from their eyes to their mouths. Leopards don't have stripes on their faces.

Cheetah   Leopard

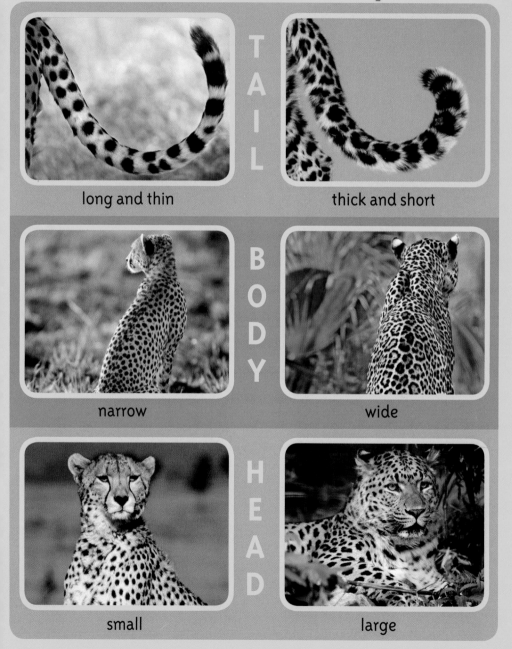

TAIL

long and thin   thick and short

BODY

narrow   wide

HEAD

small   large

Safari Speedster

In a race between a lion, a greyhound dog, and a cheetah, which animal would win?

The cheetah, hands down!

The cheetah is the fastest land animal on Earth. It can reach a running speed of 60 miles an hour in just three seconds. That's as fast as a sports car!

What makes a cheetah so fast?
Its body is built for speed.

A long tail balances the cheetah when it makes sudden, sharp turns.

A flexible spine helps it change direction quickly.

Long legs help it run fast.

A thin, lean body helps it move quickly.

Word Bites

PREY: An animal that is eaten by another animal

Excellent eyesight makes spotting prey quick and easy.

Large nostrils let it breathe easily after running.

A small head makes the cheetah lighter.

Its claws don't completely pull back into its paws like other cats. The claws grip the ground when running, like cleats on a shoe.

Its deep chest makes breathing easier while running.

Great Hunters

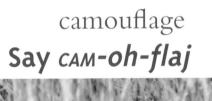

camouflage
Say *CAM-oh-flaj*

Cheetahs are sneaky when they hunt! Their spotted coats act as camouflage in tall grass. They stalk their prey slowly and quietly.

When they get close, cheetahs chase their prey.

But cheetahs get tired quickly. Whew! They need to rest, too.

How Cheetahs Live

Most cheetahs live in Africa. A very small number may still live in Iran, a country in Asia.

Like people, cheetahs can live in different habitats. Cheetahs live on the savanna and in areas with lots of plants. They also live on grasslands and in the mountains.

But cheetahs can't live near crowded buildings. They need open space.

Word Bites

HABITAT: The place where a plant or animal naturally lives

SAVANNA: A grassy plain with few trees in a hot, dry area

No matter where they live, male cheetahs stick together. Brothers live in a group called a coalition.

Female cheetahs live alone, except when caring for their cubs. Male and female cheetahs come together to have cubs. Then they live apart again.

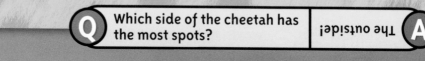

coalition
Say koh-ah-LISH-un

Cubs

A mother cheetah has three to five cubs at one time. They are born blind and helpless.

But the cubs grow quickly! They can open their eyes and crawl in less than ten days.

The mother cheetah keeps the cubs safe in their den. If she needs to move, she carries them in her mouth.

Can you find the cheetah cubs?

The cubs' dark coats blend in with the shadows. The long, soft hair along their backs looks like the dry, dead grass.

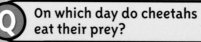

Q On which day do cheetahs eat their prey?

A Chewsday!

The cubs are protected by camouflage. It's hard for predators to find them.

Word Bites

PREDATOR: An animal that hunts and eats other animals

Playing Around

The cubs learn a lot from their brothers and sisters. They wrestle, stalk, and chase one another.

They practice skills they will need for hunting when they grow up.

When the cubs are older, the mother cheetah teaches them to hunt. She also shows the cubs which predators to avoid.

Royal Cats

Cheetahs have lived on Earth for a long, long time. As far back as ancient Egypt, pharaohs kept cheetahs as pets.

The famous pharoah King Tut was buried with many statues of cheetahs.

Statues of cheetahs from King Tut's tomb

Some ancient Egyptians believed in a cat-goddess called Mafdet. They thought Mafdet could protect the pharaohs.

Art from ancient Egypt shows cheetahs on statues, furniture, and in paintings.

Mafdet
Say MAHF-**det**

Golden head of a cheetah found in King Tut's tomb

25

Cheetah Talk

Cheetahs make sounds that tell how they're feeling. Cheetahs can't roar like other big cats. But they can purr like a house cat.

Here's a dictionary for understanding cheetah talk:

Bleating:
A cheetah bleats when it's upset. It sounds like a cat's meow.

Purring:
This is a low, motor-like sound, made when a cheetah is happy or content.

Hissing:
When a cheetah feels angry or threatened, it may let out a sharp "h" sound.

Chirping:
Cheetahs chirp when they look for each other. The call sounds like a chirping bird.

Churring or stuttering:
During social meetings, cheetahs growl with a high pitch that stops and starts.

Growling:
A cheetah growls when it feels angry or threatened.

Saving Cheetahs

You need space to run, to jump, and to play—and so do cheetahs.

More people and more buildings push cheetahs onto smaller pieces of land. Cheetahs need lots of open space to live, to hunt, and to have babies.

Less open space means cheetahs are disappearing. Today fewer than 12,000 cheetahs live in the wild.

But some people are working to save cheetahs. And we are learning more about these big cats.

The more we know, the better chance we have to keep cheetahs on Earth.

Glossary

CAMOUFLAGE: An animal's natural color or form that allows it to blend in with its surroundings

HABITAT: The place where a plant or animal naturally lives

PREDATOR: An animal that hunts and eats other animals

PREY: An animal that is eaten by another animal

SAVANNA: A grassy plain with few trees in a hot, dry area

STALK: To move secretly toward something